Step-by-step

Cooking is Easy

Step-by-step

Cooking is Easy

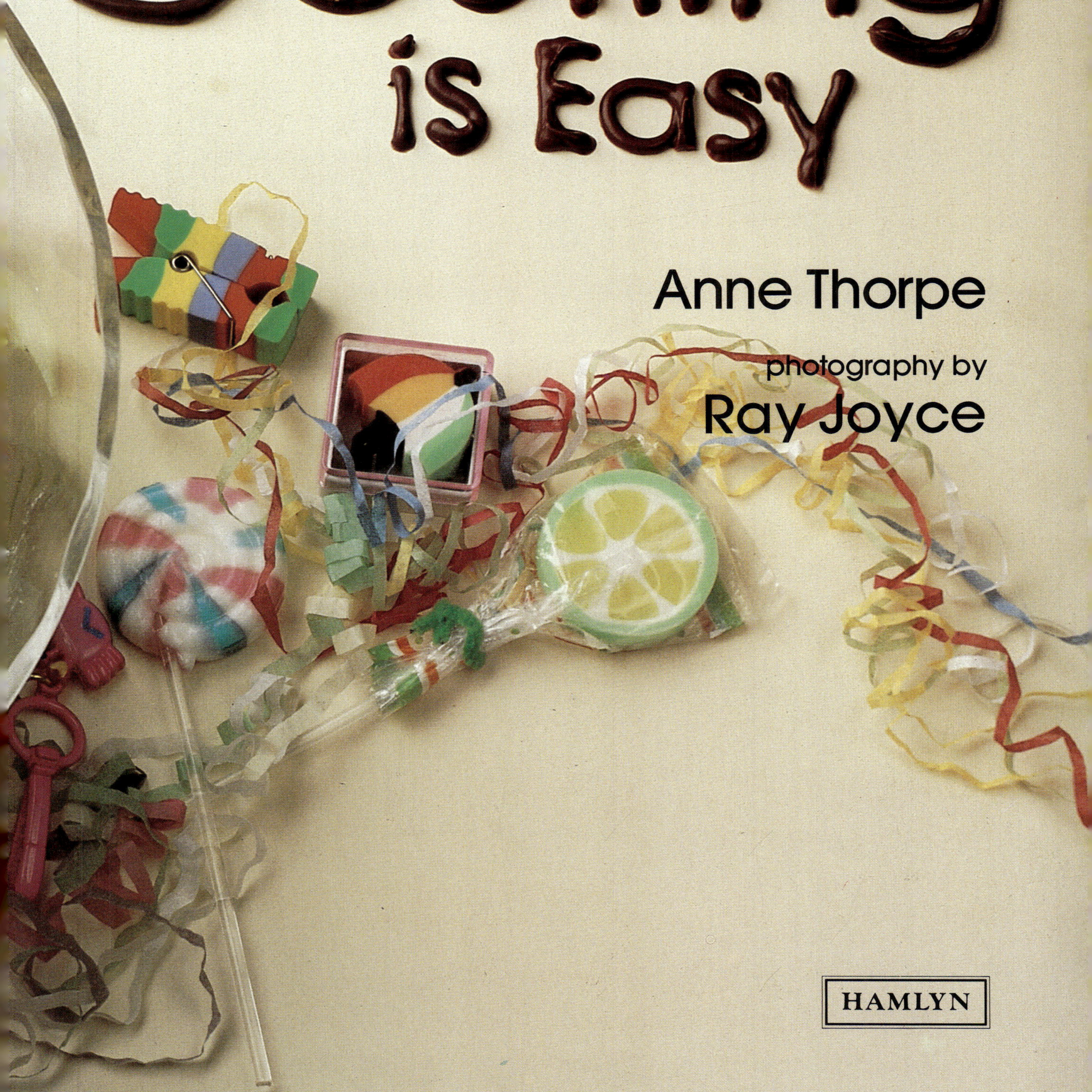

Anne Thorpe

photography by

Ray Joyce

HAMLYN

DEDICATION

For my father, Harold Vaughan, whose love of young people and simple good food brought joy to us all.

NOTES FOR COOKS

1. NEVER start cooking when you are alone in the house and ALWAYS ask permission to use the kitchen.
2. ALWAYS use a wooden chopping board for cutting.
3. ALWAYS use a heatproof stand for hot saucepans and casserole dishes.
4. Remember to read right through the recipe BEFORE starting to cook.
5. When you are chopping food WATCH OUT for your fingers.
6. Use small knives, they are easier to handle.
7. Make sure that all pot handles are turned away from the edge of the stove where they could be pulled or knocked over. Keep all handles away from spots where they could get hot.
8. ALWAYS ask an adult to pour boiling liquid out of or into a saucepan.
9. ALWAYS use a dry pot holder when handling hot containers. WET pot holders let the heat through.
10. NEVER use an electric mixer, blender or food processor unless an adult is helping you.
11. Make sure you turn off all switches and knobs after cooking.
12. Clean up AS YOU GO. It makes the job easier and safer and Mum much happier.

Our thanks to Villeroy and Boch, Wedgwood and Mark Darling Pty. Ltd. for providing the china and cutlery used in this book.

Published 1986 by Hamlyn Publishing,
a division of The Hamlyn Publishing Group Ltd.,
Bridge House, London Road, Twickenham, Middlesex, England.
By arrangement with Lansdowne Press

Printed by Pyung Hwa Dang Printing Co., Ltd. Korea.

ISBN 0 600 31114 7

CONTENTS

Beef	6
Potatoes	8
Rice and Pasta	10
Salads	12
Crêpes	14
Cakes	16
Pastry	20
Scones and Muffins	22
Sweet Treats	24
Microwave Cooking	
Chicken	26
Eggs	28
Apples	30
Chocolate	32
Index	32

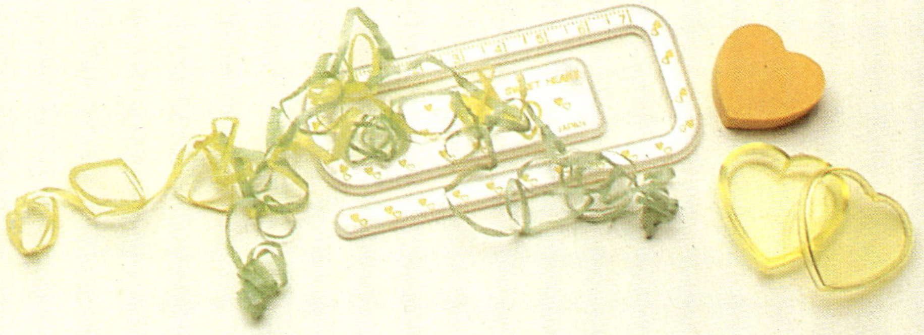

Kebabs

Serves 4

This is what you need
1 kg (2 lb) rump steak
2 medium onions
1 red pepper (capsicum)
1 green pepper (capsicum)
1 small pineapple
4 mushrooms

Marinade
1 tablespoon oil
1 clove garlic, crushed
1 tablespoon red jam (not strawberry)
1 teaspoon sugar
2 tablespoons soy sauce
2 tablespoons wine (optional)

This is what you use
cutting board
sharp knife
large bowl
kebab skewers
pastry brush

This is what you do

Step 1

Remove all the fat from the meat and cut into 2.5 cm (1 inch) cubes.

Step 2

Mix all the marinade ingredients in a large bowl. Add the steak cubes and stir gently. Leave for at least 4 hours.

Step 3

Peel the onions and cut in half. Separate the portions. Slice the peppers in half and remove the seeds. Cut the flesh into 2.5 cm (1 inch) squares. Peel the pineapple and cut into quarters. Remove the core and slice each quarter. Wipe the mushrooms and trim off the stems.

Step 4

Drain the meat and KEEP THE MARINADE. Thread the meat, onion, peppers and pineapple onto the skewers alternately and finish with a mushroom cap on each skewer.

Step 5

Cook under a hot grill (broiler) for about 7 minutes or until done, turning often and brushing with the marinade. They can also be cooked on a barbecue.
If the skewers are all metal BE CAREFUL and use oven gloves when turning them.

Baked or Barbecued French Loaf

Serves 4-6

This is what you need

1 tablespoon oil
1 small onion, finely chopped
225 g (8 oz) minced steak (ground beef)
1 long French loaf
1 large tomato, sliced
100 g (4 oz) grated cheese
50 g (2 oz) butter or margarine
1 clove garlic, crushed

This is what you use

medium frying pan
sharp knife
aluminium foil
small bowl
spoon

This is what you do

Step 1

Turn oven to 180°C (350°F/Gas 4). Pour the oil into the pan and place on medium heat. Place the onion in the pan and cook until it is transparent.

Step 2

Put the meat in the pan and continue to cook, stirring occasionally until all the meat is brown.

Step 3

Slice the French loaf along one side and pull out the soft centre. Crumble the centre dough into small pieces. Mix with the meat mixture.

Step 4

Spoon the meat into the loaf and cover with the sliced tomato and grated cheese. Press the edges of the loaf together.

Step 5

Melt the butter or margarine with the crushed garlic and spread over the loaf. Wrap in foil, sealing well. Bake on the centre shelf of the oven for 20-25 minutes or over a barbecue for 15 minutes, turning often. Serve in thick slices.

Stuffed Potatoes

Serves 6-8

This is what you need

2 bacon rashers
4 large potatoes
2 eggs
salt and pepper
milk
50 g (2 oz) grated cheese

This is what you use

small brush
skewer or fork
sharp knife
baking dish
spoon
small bowl
potato masher

This is what you do

Step 1

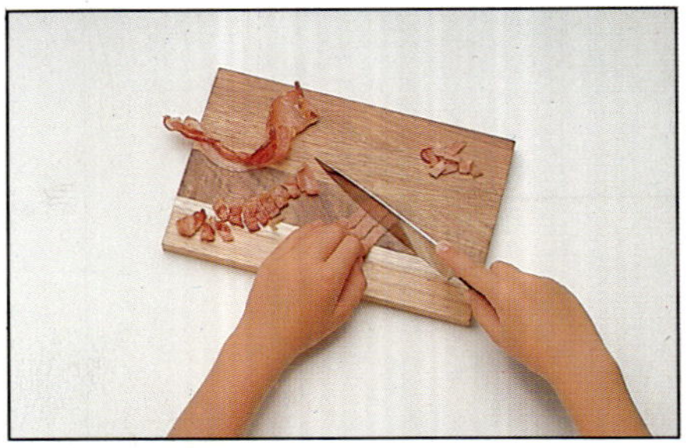

Cut the rind from the bacon and then grill (broil) on high heat until the bacon is beginning to crisp. Cut into tiny pieces.

Step 2

Turn the oven to 200°C (400°F/Gas 6). Scrub the potatoes under running water. Dry well and prick them with a skewer or fork. Place on the centre shelf of the oven for 1¾-2 hours.

At the end of the cooking time and USING OVEN GLOVES remove the potatoes from the oven and cut them in half.

Step 3

Scoop out the inside of the potato halves without breaking the skin and put in a small bowl. Mash well. Break the eggs into the potato and add salt and pepper. Mix well.

Add the bacon pieces and just enough milk to make smooth mashed potato.

Step 4

Place the potato shells in a baking dish. Spoon the filling back into the shells. It will have to be mounded up to fit the shells. Sprinkle with grated cheese and put back in the oven for 10 minutes or until the cheese is golden.

Poached Potatoes

Serves 6-8

This is what you need

1 kg (2 lb) potatoes
salt and pepper
milk
100 g (4 oz) grated cheese

This is what you use

shallow baking dish
sharp knife

This is what you do

Step 1

Turn the oven to 180°C (350°F/Gas 4). Lightly grease the baking dish. Peel the potatoes and slice them finely.

Step 2

Place the potato slices in layers in the dish and sprinkle lightly with salt and pepper between each layer.

Step 3

Pour enough milk over the potatoes to cover the bottom of the dish (about 100 ml or 4 fl oz).

Step 4

Sprinkle the grated cheese over and bake on the centre shelf of the oven for 1 hour or until the top is golden.

RICE AND PASTA

Fried Rice

Serves 6

This is what you need

450 g (1 lb) cold cooked rice
2 tablespoons oil
100 g (4 oz) cooked chopped pork, chicken or ham
2 spring onions (scallions), finely chopped
425 g (15 oz) can pineapple pieces, drained
1 stick celery, chopped
100 g (4 oz) shelled prawns
1 egg
1 tablespoon soy sauce
1 tablespoon water

This is what you use

large frying pan or wok
large spoon
cup

This is what you do

Step 1

Pour the oil into the frying pan and place over medium heat. Add the meat pieces, spring onions, pineapple and celery and fry for 2 minutes.

Step 2

Add the rice and cook for 10 minutes stirring all the time or the rice will stick. Add the prawns and mix well.

Step 3

Break the egg into the cup and stir to break the yolk. Make a space in the rice mixture and tip in the egg. When the egg is nearly cooked through stir it through the rice.

Step 4

Add the soy sauce and the water and stir well. Serve hot.

Tuna Spaghetti

Serves 4-6

This is what you need

50 g (2 oz) butter or margarine
3 tablespoons plain (all-purpose) flour
475 ml (16 fl oz) milk
198 g (7 oz) can tuna, drained and flaked
425 g (15 oz) can peeled tomatoes
1 tablespoon barbecue or Worcestershire sauce
salt and pepper
450 g (1 lb) spaghetti, cooked or 450 g (1 lb) cooked rice

This is what you use

large saucepan
wooden spoon or whisk

This is what you do
Step 1

Melt the butter or margarine in the saucepan over medium heat. Remove from heat and blend in the flour until smooth.

Step 2

Add the milk and return to the heat. Stir continuously until smooth and thickened. Stirring with a whisk will help prevent the sauce going lumpy.

Step 3

Add the tuna, tomatoes, sauce, salt and pepper. Stir gently over low heat until heated through.

Serve over the hot spaghetti or rice.

Potato Mint Salad

Serves 4-6

This is what you need

1 kg (2 lb) potatoes
1 onion, finely chopped
2 tablespoons finely chopped mint
175-275 ml (6-8 fl oz) mayonnaise

This is what you use

large saucepan
fine skewer
small knife
large salad bowl

This is what you do

Step 1

Wash the potatoes and if large, cut into pieces. Place in the saucepan and just cover with water. Boil rapidly, uncovered, over high heat for 20 minutes or until tender when pierced with a fine skewer. Carefully rinse the potatoes under running water then leave to cool.

Gently peel the skins off the potatoes and discard. Cut the potatoes into 5 mm (1/4 inch) cubes.

Step 2

Place in the bowl with the onion and mint. Add the mayonnaise and toss very gently until the potato is coated. Cover and refrigerate until ready to serve.

Marshmallow Salad

Serves 4-6

This is what you need

2 navel oranges
2 large apples
425 g (15 oz) can unsweetened pineapple pieces or
225 g (8 oz) diced fresh pineapple
100 g (4 oz) seedless white grapes
or
2 kiwi fruit
2 bananas, sliced
225 g (8 oz) packet marshmallows
250 ml (8 fl oz) natural yoghurt
3 tablespoons grated fresh coconut

This is what you use

cutting board
sharp knife
large salad bowl

This is what you do

Step 1

Peel the oranges and cut into small pieces. Place in the salad bowl.

Step 2

Cut the unpeeled apples into quarters and remove the core. Cut into small pieces. Place in the salad bowl.

Drain the pineapple and place in the bowl. Stir gently.

Add the seedless grapes or peel and slice the kiwi fruit and add these with the sliced bananas or any fruit available and stir through.

Step 3

Stir the marshmallows through the fruit mixture. Try not to eat too many.

Step 4

Spoon the yoghurt and coconut into the salad. Stir gently to mix. Serve with the main meal, not just as a dessert.

CRÊPES

Plain Crêpes

Makes 8

This is what you need

100 g (4 oz) plain (all-purpose) flour
1 egg
250 ml (8 fl oz) milk
butter or margarine

This is what you use

electric blender, food processor or medium bowl and hand beater
shallow 15 cm (6 inch) frying pan
pastry brush
egg slice or palette knife

This is what you do

Step 1

Combine the ingredients in the blender, food processor or bowl and mix well until smooth.

Step 2

Heat the pan over medium heat and brush with a little butter or margarine. Stir the mixture and pour enough batter in the middle of the pan to barely cover a 10 cm (4 inch) circle (about 2 tablespoons).

Step 3

Quickly rotate and tilt the pan so that the batter spreads in a thin layer over the entire base. If the mixture is too thick add a little more milk to thin it.

Step 4

Cook for a few minutes and then slide the slice or knife under the crêpe and turn it over. Cook for a further 2 minutes. Lift out and place on a plate.

Continue in this manner with the remaining batter. Serve warm filled with Cheese Sauce (below) or Chocolate Sauce (below). These also taste great with ice cream or fruit and cream.

Cheese Sauce

Use in crêpes or over cauliflower, broccoli, carrots or pasta.

Makes about 600 ml (1 pint)

This is what you need

50 g (2 oz) butter or margarine
3 tablespoons plain (all-purpose) flour
600 ml (1 pint) milk
100 g (4 oz) grated cheese

This is what you use

medium saucepan
wooden spoon
whisk

(*Note:* Stirring with a whisk will help prevent the sauce going lumpy.)

This is what you do

Step 1

Place the butter or margarine in a saucepan and melt over medium heat.

Step 2

Remove from the heat and blend in the flour until smooth, then add the remaining ingredients.

Step 3

Stir continuously with the whisk over medium heat until the sauce is smooth and thick.

Chocolate Sauce

Use in crêpes or over ice cream or cream puffs

This is what you need

50 g (2 oz) dark chocolate
1 tablespoon butter or margarine
1 tablespoon plain (all-purpose) flour
150 ml (5 fl oz) water
50 g (2 oz) sugar

This is what you use

small saucepan
wooden spoon

This is what you do

Step 1

Break the chocolate into small pieces. Using the small saucepan melt the butter or margarine over medium heat. Remove from heat and stir in the flour.

Step 2

Add the water and return to the heat. Stir continuously until the mixture boils then remove from the heat and add the sugar and the chocolate. Stir well to blend.

Microwave alternative

Step 1

Place the chocolate in a medium bowl and microwave on Medium (50%) for 4 minutes, then stir.

Step 2

Blend in the flour then add the butter, water, and sugar. Microwave on Medium/High (70%) for 2 minutes then stir.

Note: If the sauce is lumpy beat gently with a hand beater.

Let the sauce cool before tasting.

Plain Cake

This is what you need

100 g (4 oz) soft butter or margarine
175 g (6 oz) caster (powdered) sugar
2 eggs
225 g (8 oz) self-raising flour
100 ml (4 fl oz) milk

This is what you use

electric mixer
sieve
metric (8 fl oz) measuring cup
medium bowl
deep square or round 20 cm (8 inch) cake tin or 23 x 13 cm (9 x 5 inch) loaf tin
greaseproof paper
oven gloves
cake rack
fine skewer

This is what you do

Step 1

Turn oven to 180°C (350°F/Gas 4). Grease the cake tin and put a piece of greaseproof paper on the bottom. Put the soft butter and sugar in the bowl of an electric mixer and beat on medium speed until the mixture is light and creamy.

Step 2

Add the eggs one at a time and beat the mixture well after adding each one.

Step 3

Sieve the flour into a bowl and then stir alternately with the milk into the cream mixture. Stir gently to combine. Pour into the prepared cake tin and smooth the top.

Step 4

Bake on the centre shelf of the oven for 45-50 minutes. At the end of the cooking time and USING OVEN GLOVES remove the cake from the oven and push a fine skewer into the centre of the cake. If it comes out clean it is cooked. If it has mixture stuck to it, return the cake to the oven for a further 5 minutes.

Note: If Dad or Mum is around ask them to do this as the quicker it is done the less chance the cake will sink in the middle. If it does sink don't worry as it tastes the same.

Step 5

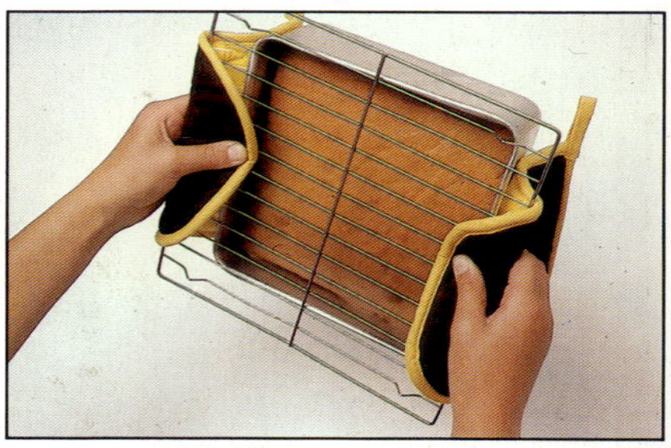

Remove the cake from the oven and leave to cool a few minutes. Now place a cake rack upside down on top of the cake and turn them over together. Carefully remove the cake tin. Leave to cool before icing.

Variations

Create an individual recipe by adding any of the following to the basic cake mixture. There are four variations given here plus some toppings, but why not try your own by substituting wholemeal flour and adding mashed

Chocolate Cake

This is what you need

Plain Cake mixture
50 ml (2 fl oz) milk
2 tablespoons cocoa

This is what you do

Step 1

Mix the milk into the cocoa until there are no lumps.

banana and chopped dates or grated carrot and walnuts. Top your cake with icing or cinnamon crumble (page 19). Remember if you add a dry, powdery ingredient you usually have to add some liquid to keep the mixture moist. Good luck!

Step 2

Stir through the cake mixture. Pour into the desired cake tin and smooth the top.

Marble Cake

This is what you need

Plain Cake mixture (page 16)
red food colouring

This is what you do

Step 1

Place half the cake mixture in a clean bowl. Stir a few drops of red food colouring into the other half. Mix through until the mixture is pale pink.

Step 2

Pour the plain half into the desired cake tin and pour in the pink half. Swirl a knife lightly through the batter to give a marble look, then smooth the top.

Sultana Tea Cake

This is what you need

Plain Cake mixture (page 16)
150 g (5 oz) sultanas
juice of 1 orange
50 g (2 oz) chopped walnuts

This is what you do

Step 1

Stir the sultanas, orange juice and walnuts through the cake mixture.

Step 2

Pour into the desired cake tin and smooth the top.

Coconut Cake

This is what you need

Plain Cake mixture (page 16)
50 g (2 oz) desiccated coconut
50 ml (2 fl oz) milk

This is what you do

Step 1

Stir the coconut and milk through the cake mixture.

Step 2

Pour into the desired cake tin and smooth the top.

Crumble Topping

Beat 50 g (2 oz) soft butter or margarine until it is creamy then add 2 tablespoons brown sugar, 1 teaspoon cinnamon and 50 g (2 oz) plain (all-purpose) flour. Mix well.

Press through a strainer or sieve onto the cake mixture or crumble with your fingers. Bake as the recipe tells you.

Pink Icing

Sieve together 225 g (8 oz) icing (confectioner's) sugar and stir in 4-6 tablespoons hot water until the icing is smooth. Stir through 2-3 drops of red food colouring. Spread on cooled cake.

Chocolate Icing

Sieve together 225 g (8 oz) icing (confectioner's) sugar and 3 tablespoons cocoa. Stir in 4-6 tablespoons hot water until the icing is smooth. Spread on cooled cake.

PASTRY

Cream Puffs

Makes 12

This is what you need

100 g (4 oz) self-raising flour
¼ teaspoon salt
2 eggs
250 ml (8 fl oz) water
50 g (2 oz) butter
whipped cream
icing (confectioner's) sugar

This is what you use

sieve
2 small bowls
medium saucepan
wooden spoon
tablespoon
baking tray
oven gloves

This is what you do

Step 1

Turn the oven to 200°C (400°F/Gas 6). Lightly grease the baking tray.

Sieve the flour and salt into a small bowl. Break the eggs into the other bowl and beat gently.

Step 2

Place the water and butter in the saucepan and bring to the boil. Remove from the heat. Add the flour and salt in one batch and stir quickly until smooth.

Step 3

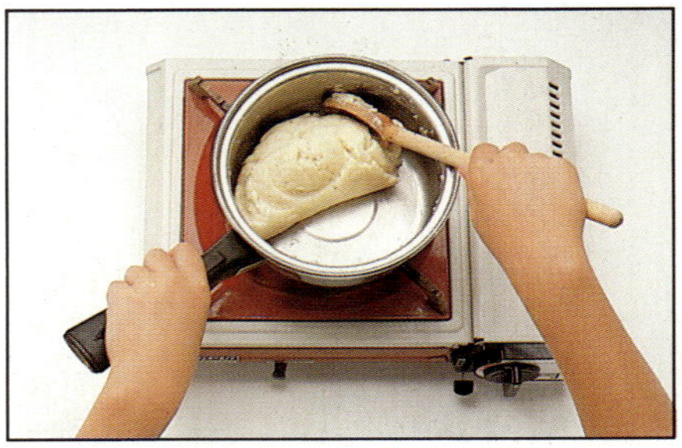

Return to the stove and stir gently over medium heat until the mixture leaves the sides of the pan (about 30 seconds). Remove from heat.

Step 4

Gradually stir in the beaten egg a little at a time until the mixture will just hold its shape. (You may not need all the egg.) Place a tablespoon at a time on the tray leaving a 5 cm (2 inch) space between.

Bake on the centre shelf of the oven for 10-12 minutes then reduce the oven temperature to 180°C (350°F/Gas 4) and continue baking for 30-35 minutes or until the puffs are crisp and dry.

Step 5

USING OVEN GLOVES remove from the oven and immediately cut open to allow the steam to escape. When cold fill with whipped cream and sprinkle with icing sugar.

Note: Serve with fresh fruit or Chocolate Sauce (page 14) may be poured over to make a rich dessert.

Quick Apple Tart

Serves 4-6

This is what you need

100 g (4 oz) self-raising flour
1 teaspoon salt
50 ml (2 fl oz) cooking oil
2-3 tablespoons cold milk
390 g (13¾ oz) can apple pie filling
crumble topping (page 19)

This is what you use

sieve
bowl
small bowl
whisk
20 cm (8 inch) flan dish

This is what you do

Step 1

Turn the oven to 200°C (400°F/Gas 6). Sieve the flour and the salt into a bowl. Pour the oil and the milk into a small bowl and whisk well.

Step 2

Pour the oil mixture into the flour and stir well to mix.

Step 3

Tip the dough into the flan dish. Press out with your fingers to cover the dish.

Step 4

Empty the apple into the pastry shell and spread evenly. Cover the apple with crumble topping and bake for 20-25 minutes or until the topping is brown and melted. Serve with whipped cream or ice cream.

SCONES AND MUFFINS

Scones

Makes 12-15

This is what you need

225 g (8 oz) self-raising flour
pinch salt
1 teaspoon sugar
25 g (1 oz) very hard butter
150 ml (¼ pint) milk or water

This is what you use

baking tray
sieve
large bowl
grater
knife
scone cutter
pastry brush

This is what you do

Step 1

Turn the oven to 230°C (450°F/Gas 8). Lightly grease the tray. Sieve the flour, salt and sugar into a large bowl.

Step 2

Grate the butter into the flour and mix through with a knife. Rub in any lumps with your fingertips.

Step 3

Add the milk and mix with a knife to form a soft sticky dough.

Step 4

Tip the mixture onto a lightly floured bench top and using your fingertips, knead gently until the dough is smooth and elastic.

Step 5

Press the dough out lightly to a thickness of about 1.5 cm (¾ inch). Dip the cutter in the flour and cut as many scones as possible.

Place on the tray very close together but not touching. Knead the remaining dough and cut more scones. Place on the baking tray.

Step 6

Lightly brush the tops of the scones with milk. Place on the centre shelf of the oven and bake for 12-15 minutes until golden-brown on top.
Note: 50 g (2 oz) of dried fruit may be added to the dry mixture.

Breakfast Muffins

Makes 12-15

This is what you need

100 g (4 oz) self-raising flour
75 g (3 oz) plain (all-purpose) flour
2 level teaspoons baking powder
50 g (2 oz) sugar
½ teaspoon salt
1 large egg
250 ml (8 fl oz) milk
3 tablespoons oil (not olive oil)

This is what you use

large bowl
wooden spoon
medium bowl
whisk
muffin or patty tins

This is what you do

Step 1

Turn the oven to 230°C (450°F/Gas 8). Grease the muffin or patty tins. Place all the dry ingredients in a large bowl and mix well.

Step 2

Place the egg, milk and oil in a medium bowl and lightly whisk.

Step 3

Pour the milk mixture into the flour and stir quickly until the mixture is wet. Do not worry about lumps.

Step 4

Place a tablespoon of mixture in each tin and bake for 20 minutes until golden-brown. Serve hot with butter and jam.

Sugar Cooking

These sweets are made by boiling sugar. This is VERY DANGEROUS as boiling sugar is hotter than boiling water and it sticks to you if you spill it. Don't make these unless Dad or Mum are with you to do all the lifting and pouring of boiling sugar.

Toffee

Makes approximately 24

This is what you need

675 g (1½ lb) sugar
250 ml (8 fl oz) water
2 teaspoons white vinegar
1 teaspoon cream of tartar
hundreds and thousands
desiccated coconut

This is what you use

large heavy saucepan
wooden spoon
small pastry brush
paper cake cases

This is what you do

Step 1

Put all the ingredients in the saucepan. Heat over a very low heat, stirring very gently with a wooden spoon to dissolve the sugar.

Step 2

Dip the brush in cold water and wash down the sides of the saucepan to remove any grains of sugar. (Undissolved grains will cause the toffee to go sugary.)

Step 3

When the sugar has dissolved DO NOT STIR AGAIN. (Stirring after the mixture has boiled will cause the toffee to go sugary.) Bring the mixture to the boil and boil for 5-8 minutes. The time will depend on the size of the saucepan. The smaller the saucepan or the heavier, the longer it will take to evaporate.

As soon as the mixture becomes pale golden-brown around the edge remove from the heat.

Step 4

Leave until the mixture stops bubbling. Carefully pour the toffee into paper cake cases and sprinkle with hundreds and thousands or coconut and leave to cool. Mum or Dad will be a great help when pouring toffee.

Peanut Brittle

This is what you need

100 g (4 oz) shelled peanuts
1 batch toffee (see opposite)

This is what you use

baking tray

This is what you do

Step 1

Grease the tray and spread the peanuts over it.

Step 2

Pour the toffee over the nuts and leave to set. When cold break into bite-sized pieces.

Yoghurt Chicken

Serves 4 *Microwave*

This is what you need

1 kg (2 lb) chicken pieces
250 ml (8 fl oz) natural yoghurt
1 clove garlic, crushed
½ teaspoon turmeric
¼ teaspoon mace
¼ teaspoon ground ginger

This is what you use

shallow casserole dish (not metal)
small bowl
spoon
fine skewer

This is what you do

Step 1

Place the chicken pieces, skin side up, in the dish.

Step 2

Put all the remaining ingredients in a small bowl and stir gently.

Step 3

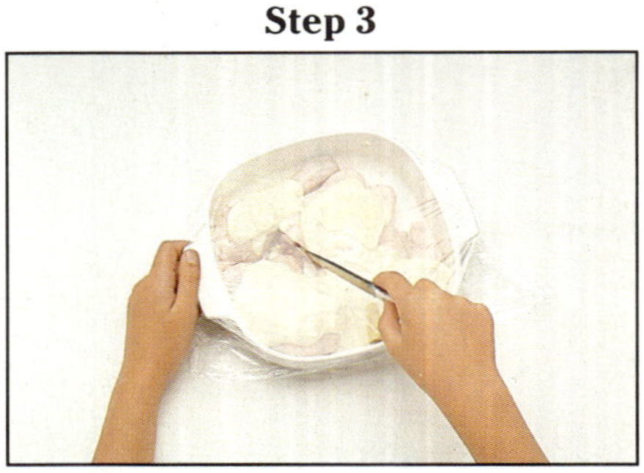

Pour the yoghurt mixture over the chicken pieces. Spoon some over each piece if not well covered. Cover with plastic wrap and cut a steam vent.

Step 4

Put the dish in the microwave and cook on Medium/High (70%) for 15-20 minutes. Pierce the chicken with a fine skewer next to the bone and if the juice runs clear the chicken is cooked. If the juice is pink cook the chicken for another 2 minutes and test again to see if it is cooked. This is delicious either hot or cold. Great for picnics.

Chinese Chicken Wings

Serves 4 *Microwave*

This is what you need

2 tablespoons golden syrup
1 tablespoon soy sauce
1 clove garlic, crushed
1 teaspoon lemon juice
1 kg (2 lb) chicken wings

This is what you use

small bowl
shallow glass or ceramic dish
spoon

This is what you do

Step 1

Place all the ingredients except the chicken wings in a small bowl. Mix well.

Step 2

Place the chicken wings in the dish. Spoon the marinade over the wings. Leave for at least 1 hour.

Step 3

Cover with plastic wrap and cut a steam vent. Place the dish in the microwave oven and cook on Medium/High (70%) for 20 minutes. If the microwave does not have a turntable rotate the dish half a turn after 10 minutes. Serve hot or cold.

EGGS

Scrambled Eggs

Serves 4 *Microwave*

This is what you need

4 eggs
4 tablespoons milk

This is what you use

medium bowl
whisk
wooden spoon

This is what you do

Step 1

Break the eggs into the bowl and add the milk. Whisk gently until the mixture is frothy.

Step 2

Place in the microwave and cook on High (100%) for 2 minutes. Stir the mixture and rotate the bowl half a turn.

Step 3

Microwave on High (100%) for another 2 minutes. Remove and stir. Serve with hot buttered toast.

Egg Custard

Serves 6 *Microwave*

This is what you need

1 litre (1¾ pints) milk
6 eggs
75 g (3 oz) sugar
ground nutmeg

This is what you use

large jug or bowl (not metal)
medium bowl
hand beater
mixing spoon
6 ramekins or custard cups

This is what you do

Step 1

Pour the milk into the jug and place in the microwave on High (100%) for approximately 5 minutes or until there are small bubbles around the edge. DO NOT BOIL.

Step 2

Break the eggs into the bowl and add the sugar. Beat well together.

Step 3

Tip the eggs into the hot milk and gently stir. Pour the milk mixture over the back of a spoon into the ramekins. This mixes the egg well.

Step 4

Sprinkle the nutmeg over the top. Place the ramekins in a circle in the microwave. Cook on Medium/High (70%) for 13 minutes. If the microwave does not have a turntable then rotate the ramekins half a turn after 7 minutes then cook for the remaining 6 minutes. The mixture MUST NOT BOIL. Let stand for a few minutes. Serve hot or cold.

Poached Eggs

erves 4 *Microwave*

This is what you need

4 eggs

This is what you use

small cups or microwave egg dish
plastic wrap suitable for microwave

This is what you do

Step 1

3reak the eggs into the cups or dish
ınd cover each with plastic wrap.

Step 2

Aicrowave on Medium/High (70%) for
:-2½ minutes or until the egg white is
10 longer clear. Let stand for a few
ninutes before removing the wrap.

Serve on hot buttered toast.

Note: If you continue to cook the
eggs, they will explode.

Variations

Gently stir the eggs in the cups to break he yolk, then add a little chopped ham, bacon, grated cheese or finely chopped spring onions. Cover the eggs with plastic wrap and nicrowave as shown above.

APPLES

Baked Apples

Serves 4 *Microwave*

This is what you need

4 large Granny Smith or red cooking apples
butter
golden syrup

This is what you use

small sharp knife or apple corer
plastic or ceramic dish
teaspoon

This is what you do

Step 1

Remove the core from the apples by cutting down and around the stem, then down and around from the base of the apple. Push the core out.

Step 2

Make a cut only through the skin, one-third down the side of the apple, and all the way round.

Step 3

Place the apples in the dish. Spoon a small knob of butter into each hole and push halfway down. Place a teaspoonful of golden syrup in the hole on top of the butter.

Step 4

Place the dish in the microwave oven and cook on High (100%) for 6 minutes. If the microwave does not have a turntable then rotate the dish half a turn after 3 minutes then cook for the remaining 3 minutes.

Remove the dish from the oven and place on individual serving plates.

Step 5

Spoon any juice in the dish over the apples.

Savoury Baked Apples

Serves 4 *Microwave*

This is what you need

4 Granny Smith or red cooking apples
1 small onion, finely chopped
cooked ham or bacon, finely chopped
grated cheese

This is what you use

small sharp knife or apple corer
small bowl
teaspoon
plastic or ceramic dish

This is what you do

Step 1

Remove the core from the apples (see recipe opposite) and place in the dish. Mix together the onion and the ham or bacon

Step 2

Stuff the mixture down the centre of the apples. Pack the filling well down and mound a little on top. Microwave on High (100%) for 6 minutes. If the microwave does not have a turntable then rotate the dish half a turn after 3 minutes then cook for the remaining 3 minutes.

Step 3

Remove from the oven and sprinkle with grated cheese. Microwave again on High (100%) for 1 minute to melt the cheese. Serve as a snack or with a barbecue or roast pork.

CHOCOLATE

Chocolate Clusters

Makes 12 *Microwave*

This is what you need

100 g (4 oz) dark, milk or white chocolate
100 g (4 oz) crushed toffee (page 24)
Note: Crush in a food processor or in a plastic bag with a rolling pin
or
100 g (4 oz) shelled peanuts
or
100 g (4 oz) sultanas
or
100 g (4 oz) chopped dates

This is what you use

small bowl
wooden spoon
baking tray

This is what you do

Step 1

Break the chocolate into small pieces and microwave on Medium (50%) for 3 minutes, then stir. Return to the microwave for 20 seconds at a time if it is not melted.

Step 2

Stir one of the remaining ingredients through the melted chocolate and place spoonfuls on the tray. Leave to set.

INDEX

Baked Apples 30
Baked or Barbecued French Loaf 7
Breakfast Muffins 22
Cheese Sauce 14
Chinese Chicken Wings 26
Chocolate Cake 16
Chocolate Clusters 32
Chocolate Icing 19
Chocolate Sauce 14
Coconut Cake 18
Cream Puffs 20
Crumble Topping 19
Egg Custard 28
Fried Rice 10
Kebabs 6
Marble Cake 17
Marshmallow Salad 13
Peanut Brittle 25
Pink Icing 19
Plain Cake 16
Plain Crêpes 14
Poached Eggs 29
Poached Potatoes 9
Potato Mint Salad 12
Quick Apple Tart 20
Savoury Baked Apples 30
Scones 22
Scrambled Eggs 28
Stuffed Potatoes 8
Sultana Tea Cake 18
Toffee 24
Tuna Spaghetti 10
Yoghurt Chicken 26

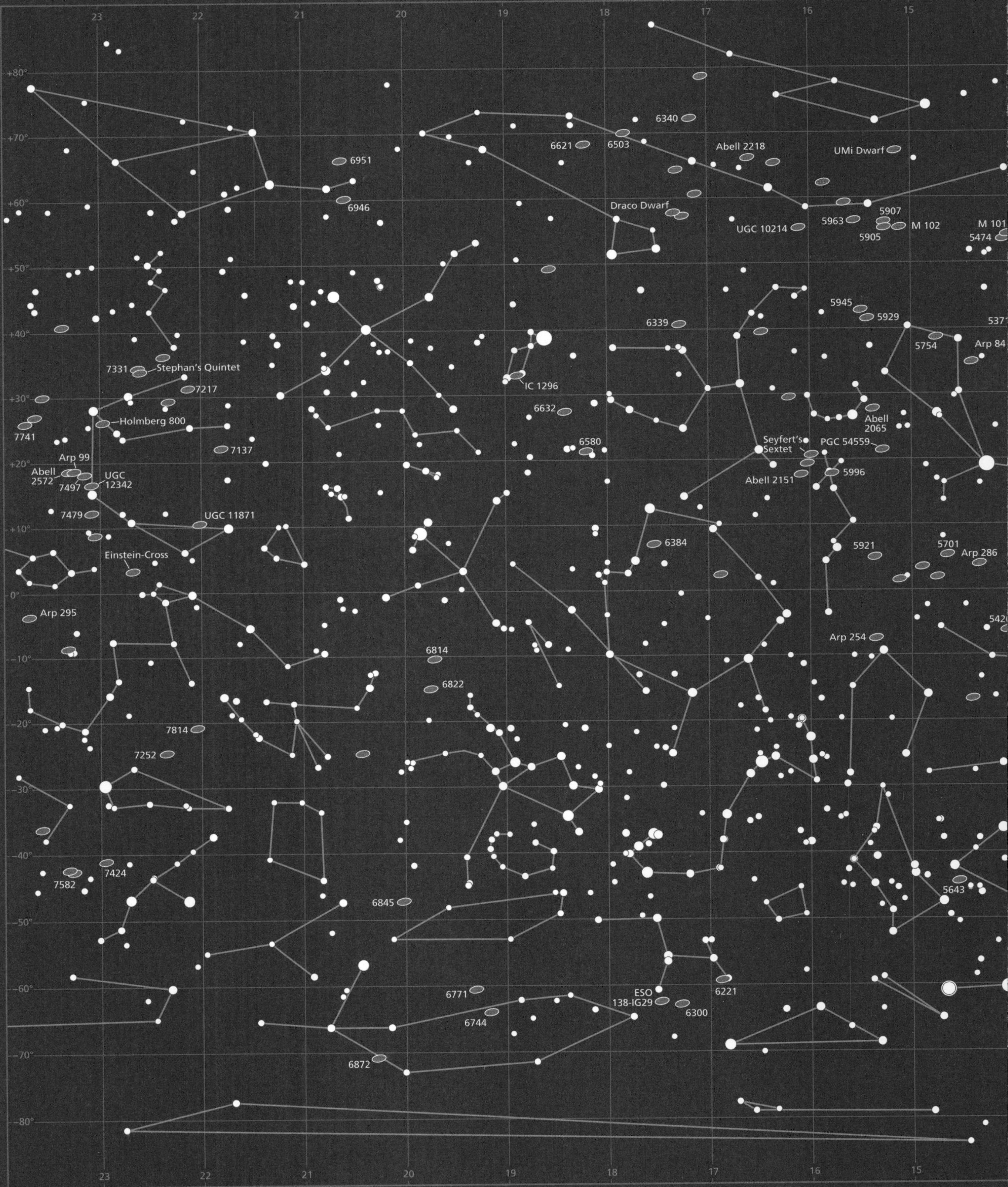

23
22
21
20
19
18
17
16
15
+80°
+70°
+60°
+50°
+40°
+30°
+20°
+10°
0°
-10°
-20°
-30°
-40°
-50°
-60°
-70°
-80°
6340
6621
6503
Abell 2218
UMi Dwarf
6951
6946
Draco Dwarf
UGC 10214
5963
5907
5905
M 102
M 101
5474
5945
5929
6339
5754
Arp 84
7331
Stephan's Quintet
IC 1296
7217
6632
Abell 2065
Holmberg 800
7741
6580
7137
Seyfert's Sextet
PGC 54559
Arp 99
Abell 2572
7497
UGC 12342
Abell 2151
5996
7479
UGC 11871
6384
5921
5701
Arp 286
Einstein-Cross
Arp 295
Arp 254
6814
6822
7814
7252
7424
7582
5643
6845
6771
ESO 138-IG29
6221
6300
6744
6872